$\mathscr{T}$his book belongs to:

Jeannie G Zuxe

$\mathscr{F}$rom:

Mrs R Ncele

$\mathscr{D}$ate:

_a — o 09 - 11 -03_

SOUL-FOOD *for* LIFE'S *Road*

Nic Wiehahn

Christian Art Gifts

SOUL-FOOD FOR LIFE'S ROAD
Prof. Nic Wiehahn

Originally broadcast as a regular feature on the radio station
Radiosondergrense (RSG) under the title *Nic se Rubriek*
Copyright © 1998-1999 by Nic Wiehahn

Published by Christian Art, PO Box 1599,
Vereeniging 1930, South Africa

© 1999
First edition 2000

Designed by Christian Art
Original Afrikaans version adapted and edited by Althéa Kotze
Translated by Joan Lötter

Unless otherwise indicated, all Scripture quotations
are taken from the *Holy Bible,* New International
Version®. NIV®. Copyright © 1973, 1978, 1984 by
International Bible Society. Used by permission of
Zondervan Publishing House. All rights reserved.

ISBN 1-86852-697-6

Printed and bound in Singapore

00 01 02 03 04 05 06 07 08 09 – 10 9 8 7 6 5 4 3 2 1

Contents

Foreword
About the author   9

1. Question mark or note of exclamation   11
2. The value of a good fright   15
3. The role of criticism in our lives   19
4. Mistakes, reproaches,
   accusations and forgiveness   24
5. Prosperity and adversity   29
6. It is better to remember than not to forget   34
7. Positive thinking   39
8. Self-faith and self-confidence   47
9. The human tongue   52
10. Remorse, self-reproach and self-crucifixion   57
11. Fear and anguish   61
12. From retaliation to reconciliation   65
13. Change   71
14. Loneliness and isolation   76

Foreword

The three books in this range contain the first two series of talks on life's values that I presented over the past two years on the radio station *Radiosondergrense* (RSG) on the programme *Forum*.

I have always been interested in life's values, probably because the qualities they represent appeal to my personality. Firstly, they are usually short and to the point. Secondly, and perhaps more importantly, they are always true to life. This element of truth distinguishes them from other types of descriptions and sayings. Truth is like a cork or an air bubble – it cannot be kept down, it always surfaces, even if it takes a while. In the third place, most of life's values have universal appeal, thus they can be expressed in any language. In the fourth place, these qualities keep life's values alive and relevant and so they are passed on from generation to generation, and even from one civilisation to another.

I find life's values a source of blessing, inspiration and empathy. They contain the wisdom of ages and serve the purpose of a compass in our uncertain voyage on the stormy seas of life – they give direction and peace of mind.

This is why I started my collection of values, sometimes creating my own, because at some stage, all of us try to put into words the truth or value of a situation or a quality in someone or something as it appears to us. Should the description be true and, moreover, a universal truth, it becomes a value of life; it is remembered and passed on to future generations.

Life's values are not restricted to a particular language; they can be expressed equally well in almost any language and every idiom. This explains, to a certain extent, why a particular value is ascribed to a certain author in one source, only to be quoted in another as the words of wisdom of a different, often earlier author. This, however, is not a problem. In the end the value of a quotation is determined by the truth it holds and its universal relevance, not by the author.

I trust that the reader of these books will experience the same joy and blessing I experienced when writing my radio talks on life's values. The truth of life that we carry deep in our hearts is the true source of love, joy and happiness.

In conclusion, and without mentioning any names, I would like to express my heartfelt thanks and appreciation to *Radiosondergrense,* the producer, presenter, the publishers and to every person who made the publication of these books possible.

~ *Prof. Nic Wiehahn* ~

---

* The talks reproduced in this volume are the first in a series of three gift books compiled from the original *Nic se Rubriek,* broadcast on the radio station *Radiosondergrense.*

About the author

*N*icholas Everhardus Wiehahn – or just Prof. Nic, as he is affectionately known – was born in Mafikeng. He matriculated from Diamantveld High School at the age of 21, after leaving school twice. With a mischievous glint in the eye he remembers: "That year I was the oldest school pupil in the Cape Province. When I walked into the matric class in March 1949, the headmaster promptly asked me to shave off my moustache."

He studied part-time and was awarded the B.A. and LL.B. degrees, after which he was called to the bar as advocate of the Supreme Court. After extensive research at various universities and institutes in Europe, America and the East, he was awarded a doctorate in law. He subsequently specialized in labour law and labour relations in South Africa. His name is associated with many commissions of enquiry that he has led, and will most certainly be noted in the annals of South African history.

Perseverance, determination, hard work, and limitless faith in himself have all contributed to the meteoric success of his career, and have ultimately gained him worldwide recognition and various awards. As a public speaker both locally and abroad, he is often introduced as "a pioneer in his country, an academic, advocate, businessman, media personality, thinker, writer and the eternal student – one of the most versatile citizens of his country, with both feet on the ground, and an eternal song in his heart."

His philosophy of life is that the secret of success is believing in yourself, because doubting success is inviting failure. To achieve success you sometimes fall, but failure is not in falling, it is in staying down. The only true helping hand is the one at the end of your own arm.

Prof. Nic's love of reading and studying is at the root of his exceptionally wide interest in the many disciplines of the human sciences: law, philosophy, history, the classics, economics and many more. From this grew his liking and love for, and interest in basic human values and he started collecting examples of such values. At the request of the radio station *Radiosondergrense* (RSG) he has already presented two series of talks on life's values in his radio programme *Nic se Rubriek*. The exceptional popularity of this programme has given rise to a request for the talks to be published in the form of a gift book such as this one.

We trust that you, the reader, will derive just as much enjoyment and inspiration from this book as the listeners of Prof. Nic's programme did.

1

Question mark or note of exclamation

*N*ot long ago a friend asked me if I had noticed how many people nowadays seem to walk about with downcast eyes or bowed head when they have occasion to appear in the streets. I had not been aware of it myself but the remark made me more observant, and I realised that too many people walking about had their heads bowed and their eyes downcast. Over the centuries a bowed head has been associated with respect, sympathy, empathy, gratitude and guilt, but also with defeat, dejection, depression and other negative or pessimistic emotions or dispositions. When looking at photos of prisoners of war the dejection is clear in their bowed postures, as if they were ashamed of their defeat. In earlier times slaves were not allowed to lift up their heads in the presence of their masters. In court the accused will usually sit with a bowed head.

My thoughts went back to one day when I was returning home from school. I was walking along the well-known way home, feeling as if I carried the world on my shoulders. My head was hanging and all I could see was the boring grey of the sidewalk. I was depressed, discouraged and apathetic. Suddenly I bumped my head against a corner-post of the bus stop. I was embarrassed and slightly stunned. Then an elderly man, who was waiting for the bus and had witnessed my little accident, spoke to me, smiling slightly and with a friendly gleam in his eye: "My boy, I saw you

> Any person who stumbles through life with a downcast head is unable to face his problems.

coming along with your head hanging low and thought that you were sure to hit the post. Now tell me, why are you walking that way and why don't you watch where you are going?"

"Oh dear me, sir," I answered, "I was thinking about all my problems and difficulties: the exams next week, lots of homework, the long way home, and so many other problems."

"So," he said laughingly, "you bumped yourself on the head and now you have a splendid egg on the forehead to show for it. Let me teach you something: one does not go through life with a hanging head and downcast eyes. You are trying to ignore your problems and the only thing that happens is that you allow your problems to push down your head so that you can't see them or those other problems on the way. You are using your eyes in the wrong way. When you drop your head like that, you only give your shoulders more room to carry problems. When you look up, you can see the beautiful things in front of you and look forward to something good – in you problems as well. Often you will realise that they are not as bad as you thought. Lift up your head and look to the future. Problems don't like a determined look in one's eye."

This short sermon has stayed with me through the years. While reading the Bible it has struck me how many references there are to one's eyes and the important role they play in human relationships and daily life. I have realised that it is no good to approach one's problems with a downcast head and dejection. No, what you need is a determined, clear look of victory.

Lyle, the poet, has written that a clear, firm look, with tiny wrinkles around the eyes making friendly curtains, is a true window to the soul. A friendly, square look from your fellow man tells both of you so much more than words. And because the eyes are more truthful than the tongue, the language spoken by the eye is eternally and universally valid. No dictionary is needed for the language of the eye. A while ago I was once again made aware of the psychological power of the eye when a blind friend told me that he had "faced his problems squarely and examined them closely to see what he could do about them."

To me it has become a universal truth that any person who stumbles through life with a downcast head is unable to face his old problems – and neither can he see the new ones com-

> Lift up your head and look to the future. Problems don't like a determined look in one's eye.

ing. But, even worse, that person is unable to see the beauty in life, nor the joy or sadness in the eyes of others. Browne wrote: "Proudly, strong and upright, head and chin up, a nation marches forth against all setbacks."

I believe that going through life with a downcast head will make you a question mark, instead of your being an exclamation mark.

> A clear, firm look, with tiny wrinkles around the eyes making friendly curtains, is a true window to the soul.
>
> *~ John Lyle ~*

2

$\mathcal{T}$he value of
a good fright

$\mathcal{M}$any authors have said that a good fright is much more valuable than any advice, admonition or warning could hope to be. This truth has been expressed in different ways by various authors. However, they agree that all people have weaknesses which they are unable to keep hidden most of the time. When you are tempted, you will give in with the firm decision and resolution: "This is the last time. As from tomorrow I will be stronger and not indulge my weakness again." We are well acquainted with our weaknesses and no matter how much good advice or warnings we are given in that regard, when temptation knocks at our door our knees turn to water once more, as Emerson so aptly remarked. Sometimes we succumb openly and at other times we try to do so in secret. For example, many people get gout from beer or wine, but keep on drinking it regardless. In the same way the dangers of smoking are brought to our attention emphatically, yet thousands of people continue smoking. There are indeed numerous examples of such human weaknesses. Sir Walter Raleigh wrote that some people would die rather than listen.

The problem is not to persuade a person that he suffers from that weakness – he knows about it only too well – but to convince him to do something about it. That is where the value of the fright comes in. Some people, as the saying goes, need to feel before they will listen!

The other day I found a story dating from the 1960s in my files. It was a news item and told of a man who had been partying too much. At long last he started home, but it was raining, a cold wind was blowing and he was extremely uncertain on his feet. He decided to

> The problem is not to persuade a person that he suffers from that weakness – he knows about it only too well – but to convince him to do something about it.

take a shortcut through a graveyard. Halfway through the graveyard, the ground suddenly gave way and he fell into a newly dug grave. Wet and dirty, he tried to get out but he kept slipping back in the wet soil. He could not get up the two-metre-deep sides either. So he decided to spend the night in the grave and tried to find the driest corner. Sitting down, he thought he might have a smoke, but his matches were wet as well. So he waited for the sun to rise and somebody to find him.

In the meantime another person also took the way through the same graveyard. Suddenly the soft ground gave way under him and he fell into the same grave. The first man welcomed the company and said: "Good evening. Do you happen to have matches on you?" Then things started to happen very quickly. Man number two took off like a rocket and somehow got out of the grave, landing a good metre outside on solid ground, then ran away as fast as he could. The partygoer was "saved" by the gravediggers next morning, very wet and absolutely miserable with a huge hangover-headache. He told his story to a newspaper who printed it and offered a reward to the other man if he would come forward to tell how he had managed the "takeoff" out of the grave.

He did tell his story in the end. He said that he was depressed, negative and discouraged because of problems in his marriage, his job and his financial situation. It had become his way of life to be negative. He had consulted psychologists but avoided them when they told him his approach was negative and warned him against it. He had decided to commit suicide, and to get used to the graveyard atmosphere, he made a habit of walking home through that one at night. He called it "the gate of my future home – the devil in hell." That night he thought that hell had opened to him and he honestly thought that it was the devil himself asking him for matches. And he didn't even have any matches!

Running home for all he was worth, he realised that life with all its problems meant more to him than he had thought and that he had not sufficiently appreciated it. This one shock changed his entire life. He started looking his problems in the face, built up new courage and accepted that he was brought to that point in his life in order to start a new life. He became deeply religious and a changed man, believing that his fall into the open grave was the only way in which the heavenly Father could bring him to his senses.

> Our knees turn to water every time temptation knocks at our door.
>
> ~ Ralph Waldo Emerson ~

3

The role of criticism in our lives

The American author Hubbard wrote that anybody who never wants to be criticised should do nothing, say nothing and be nothing, because that is the only way to be so uninteresting that you are not worth any criticism. It is but human to criticise; all of us sometimes have something to say about the actions of our fellow human beings, and we are sometimes criticised ourselves. Criticism, like conflict, cannot be avoided and it is indeed necessary. The only problem, as Nathan so aptly remarked, is that not everybody knows the difference between constructive and destructive criticism.

A further problem is that the person who criticises and the one who is criticised do not always understand the meaning of the other. The one who criticises may want to be constructive but the criticisee sees it as destructive. Quite often it is not *what* is said but *how* it is said. Emerson spoke a true word when he warned to be careful when criticising; there must be no doubt about the good will and constructive intent behind the criticism. Formulation is all-important to point the correct way without giving umbrage and to provide inspiration. Naturally the effect or result of criticism depends to a large degree on the sensitivity of the person

> Criticism, like conflict, cannot be avoided and it is indeed necessary.

who is criticised. Most people are inclined to forget positive criticism in no time. Water down a duck's back flows as fast.

However, Huneker said that, should your reaction to criticism be negative and irate, you probably deserved it! And Woodall's opinion is that, should criticism be truly damaging, the skunk would have died out many years ago. Another author, Smith, believes in a little perfume or positive spice along with the hard words – in other words, sugaring the pill. The result should be an upliftment of the spirit and nourishment for the personality.

Most authors, though acknowledging the necessity for critics in the community, are wont to condemn them or at least be most critical of them. Huneker said that most critics expect miracles, and Nathan's opinion is that critics try to share in the fame of those they criticise. Disraeli said long ago that it is much easier to be critical than correct.

Criticism usually has one of two, and sometimes both, sources. One source is jealousy, envy and even malice. Shakespeare used to call it "the green malady," which is a bad or negative source. The other is sincere interest and involvement; usually a positive source.

Knowledgeable people maintain that the first kind of criticism develops in a family or group of friends. A family member does well and surpasses his family and friends. His success leads to envy and jealousy among some of his family and friends. Guiterman is of the opinion that this situation leads to malicious and fierce criticism on the head of the successful individual. Depending on how the successful person processes the criticism, the stones flung at him may build his monument.

Each one of us is born with a God-given life that we must fill in ourselves. Should you amble through life without a goal, without ideals, without creating your opportunities and utilising them to the maximum, then your life, as Franklin put it, will be empty and aimless and then you may join the critics' brigade. You are nothing because you have accomplished nothing. And then that other beautiful truth of life kicks in: He who contributed nothing to the world by his life, will do so in death. It must be terrible to have been born, to have spent a lifetime doing ordinary prosaic things to merely keep breathing, and one day to die knowing that you have accomplished nothing; your life was empty and aimless and your sole contribution to life was criticism. That is why, said

> Quite often it is not *what* is said but *how* it is said.

Guitry, there are no monuments to critics. Washington, another author, drew a distinction between what he called "pavilion people" and "arena people." The "best" athletes, politicians, artists and others are merely spectators on the pavilion of life. They always know best how things should have been done. Their faces are always clean, eyes clear and they carry no life-wounds or spiritual injuries. They are people without legs who are teaching others to run. The arena group are those who enrich the world through their lives. They are full of wounds and injuries picked up in the arena of life. They normally have no time to criticise others. They are too involved in the daily business of life. They *live* and are not *being* lived, according to Herodotus. He also said: "It is better to be criticised than pitied."

Years ago I followed Theodore Roosevelt's view of criticism whenever jealousy, criticism and gossip had hurt me: "Expect no praise without envy and a pinch of jealousy while you are alive."

Consider the fact that honour, recognition, gratitude and appreciation are not bestowed on those who do nothing but criticise; neither on those who scornfully and with pleasure point out how many times another had stumbled or fallen, or where he might have done better in life, or where he fell short or suffered defeat.

No, that kind of honour, recognition, thanks and appreciation are due to the person who:

- without hesitation, applies his physical and spiritual powers enthusiastically to change his surroundings and situation in the arena of life for the better;
- always has his face covered in honest sweat, dust and the signs of the fight for quality life in which he is forever involved;
- is merely human in his mistakes and shortcomings;
- accepts the challenges of life enthusiastically and with excitement;

- knows about the stress and tension that comes along with dedication, sacrifices and involvement;
- at least in the end had experienced the overwhelming happiness of having reached the heights and, should he have failed, at the very least having failed in greatness and pride.

Such a person does not find his place in the row of the blind and sterile community of critics and gossipers who know neither victory nor defeat.

I should like to leave you with a truth of life spoken by Edward Wallis Hich: "There is so much good in the worst of us and so much bad in the best of us, that it hardly becomes any of us to talk about the rest of us."

> Be careful when criticising; there must be no doubt about the good will and constructive intent behind the criticism. Formulation is all-important to point the correct way without giving umbrage and to provide inspiration.
>
> ~ Ralph Waldo Emerson ~

4

$\mathscr{M}$istakes, reproaches, accusations and forgiveness

$\mathscr{I}$t is only human to err. This diction does not come from the Bible alone, but scores of authors from all times have stressed this truth. Most authors base their outlook on life on this characteristic that is shared by all human beings. Maximus said it was unthinkable that any person could go through life without ever making a mistake. Goethe agreed, writing that mankind's urge to change and improve is the reason why there will always be mistakes made by humans. Aeschylus said succinctly that even the best of us make mistakes.

A few authors differ by maintaining that there is no such thing as errors on earth. It is people's incorrect judgment that characterises certain behaviour as mistakes. The Duke of Wellington is reported to have written in a letter to a friend that, apart from the sins arising from transgression of the Ten Commandments, there is no such thing as a mistake. So-called mistakes merely arise from people's less correct decisions resulting in less or more experience of life for them. Therefore, continued the Duke, there have never been any mistakes and there never will be any. The march of history is faultless. So much for the minority viewpoint.

Apart from the fact that mistakes and faults are human and therefore unavoidable, some authors believe that there must be advantages in making mistakes or having human faults. The French author, Fraude, said that mistakes above all else are the best teachers, and Bishop Magee maintained that any human who never errs, cannot accomplish anything and indeed does not live.

An interpretation of one of Ovid's doctrines says that the aim of forgiveness is to cleanse the soul after a wrongdoing – a purification that is essential for the renewal of the spirit. With-

> Let yesterday's misdeeds be buried by yesterday.

out mistakes, forgiveness from person to person would be purposeless. Therefore faults are not only human but also necessary. A wrongdoing normally leads to a feeling of guilt in the person who committed it. Bulwer-Lytton was of the opinion that there was no greater spiritual torment than that following a wrongdoing about which we are really ashamed. That is why some people feel that only death can release them from such agony of shame. Plautus also stressed the post-agony of the perpetrator when he said that a wrongdoing may be forgiven, but the shame attached to it will live on ...

maybe forever.

However, many authors warn against the negative effects of carrying a feeling of guilt over a wrongdoing. Cicero said: "He who blames himself overly much for a mistake, commits a second misdeed," and Susan Colling advised: "Let yesterday's misdeeds be buried by yesterday." Oscar Wilde believed that one should never reproach oneself for misdeeds. Hubbard agreed, but added: "Make good!" Meuniere and Montaigne both said that he who reproaches himself for a mistake is crucifying himself, usually unnecessarily.

> Tolerance and forgiveness are the two most beautiful words after love.

Many authors accentuate the positive role played by forgiveness and its healing effect on a person. I have referred to those authors who maintain that faults are human and that they are necessary for the cleansing of the spirit. It is like water: cleansing and calming. One should of course avoid repetition of mistakes, because, as Cicero said, then the mistake becomes bigger and bigger until it becomes unforgiveable. Forgiveness will then do no more good than trying to wash clothing in dirty water.

Without forgiveness or purification the role of mistakes is incomplete. That is why one must get over the wrongdoing and cleanse oneself from the feeling of guilt. Addison wrote that one should not reproach oneself with one's mistakes. True repentance over your wrongdoings should urge you to two decisions: to take the positive aspects from it, and not to repeat the same error.

Many authors call for forgiveness of other people's misdemeanors. Bailey wrote that he who forgives, will be forgiven most; and the other way round, he who is forgiven most, will also be able to forgive most. Epictetus added: tolerance and forgiveness are the two most beautiful words after love. La Roché wrote that one forgives in the same measure that one loves. Forgiveness is an important theme in the Bible and is part of biblical prayer.

The opposite of forgiveness is revenge or reprisal. Seneca called revenge an inhuman word. Where there is true forgiveness, there is obviously no room for revenge. But it is not for us to take revenge. People who forgive, do not want revenge. That is why Pittacus said: "Forgiveness is much better than revenge," because, added Epictetus, forgiveness is a sign of love for one's neighbour, while revenge is a sign of cruelty. Syrus put it in a nutshell when he said that forgiveness is not only beautiful but it is evidence of love as well. Laurence Stone wrote that only heroes know how to forgive; it is not in a coward's makeup to forgive. Francis Bacon said that revenge kept wounds open that could become septic and lead to death.

> Revenge contradicts the principle of neighbourly love.

Robert Browning went as far as to write: "Good, to forgive; best, to forget." Both Milton and Shakespeare were convinced that the end of revenge must be tragedy and death. Revenge may be sweet at first, but it will become gall in the end.

The authors Bohn, John Ray and Samuel Palmer are convinced that forgiveness is the best way of revenge. Palmer added: "And if you can forgive with a sincere smile, it is so much better." This approach agrees with Romans 12:20: "In doing this, you will heap burning coals on his head."

I close with the truth that it is human to make mistakes, but most authors also confirm that reproach and accusations for mistakes ("if only I had" or "I told you so" or "but you said"):

- never resolved any problems;
- never made love between two people better or deeper;
- never restored peace between people;
- never repaired any damage caused by the mistake or wrongdoing;

but has always been and will always be a force that destroys relationships and, ultimately, people. Revenge contradicts the principle of neighbourly love.

> He who forgives, will be forgiven most; and the other way round, he who is forgiven most, will also be able to forgive most.
>
> ~ Philip James Bailey ~

5

*P*rosperity and adversity

*M*ankind will always strive towards prosperity, wealth and possessions because, as John Webster wrote, it is the aim of mankind to collect the wherewithal in order to be free from worries and cares. Man has a natural fear of the unknown pain and agony that a future without means may hold. However, the problem is that, as Emerson so aptly put it, man will never reach that point where he will declare: "Now I have enough prosperity, riches and possessions."

That is why, wrote Thomas Fuller, prosperity and contentment can never be friends. Burton added that wealth and contentment are seldom to be found in the same person.

Another problem, mentioned by Horace, is that man will never be satisfied

> Adversity and trials test one's faith.

as long as his neighbour has more than he has. This competitiveness is well known, also in our country and community.

Most authors paint a negative picture of prosperity,

wealth and possessions, while praising the virtues of adversity and tribulations. Danielle wrote that your problems start when your prosperity and wealth are acknowledged by your fellow men, because that is where your enemies come from. Curtius Rufus warned

> Wealth and contentment are seldom to be found in the same person.

that prosperity and wealth may change people's approach to life and other people. Few people can withstand the effect of prosperity and wealth. Carlyle declared that for every one person who was able to handle the effects of wealth and prosperity, there were hundreds who were much better at handling trials and tribulations, and Hubbard agreed by stating that the ordinary person handles problems better than wealth. Beku declared that "prosperity and wealth give free rein, destroy fools and expose the wise among us to dangers." According to Thomas Fuller, adversity is endured easier than prosperity is forgotten. Tacitus and Horace agreed that prosperity and wealth tended to corrupt people and to hide the genius and originality of man. Adversity brings it out once more.

The thought that adversity and trials test one's faith was mentioned by authors Ben Jonson, Livy and John Brown, who all wrote that adversity taught one to pray. Brown also said: "Hardship is the process used by heaven to test your virtues because trials are often the dark cloud behind which the bright sun of a shining future is hidden." Jonson declared that prosperity never taught one to pray.

Many authors tried to strike a balance between prosperity, wealth and success on the one hand and adversity, trials and poverty on the other. They condemned neither prosperity and wealth nor adversity and tribulations. Gsoeralis wrote: "One should keep in mind that in every community there will be people who are prosperous and wealthy and others who experience poverty and adversity." Few, if any communities have a perfect balance between poverty and wealth. There is always some imbalance. In a community such as South Africa's it is even more apparent, because this society is filled with extremes of rich and poor. Socrates wrote that one should not be overjoyed in times of prosperity, nor too downhearted during adversity. The author Terence offers the good advice that one should consider the bad times during your prosperous years so that you are prepared when adversity strikes. Seneca said: "Blessed is the person who can carry the burden of king and slave equally well and adapt to it, because he will be able to bear suffering and tribulations."

> Trials are often the dark cloud behind which the bright sun of a shining future is hidden.

Many authors have warned against the disadvantages of too much prosperity, wealth and success, too many to mention here. It all comes down to the fact that prosperity, success and wealth may easily lead to laziness, corruption, injustice, bribery, overprotection, infidelity, cowardice, shallowness and, above all, a dilution of the timeless, positive and beneficial values of life. According to Emerson, difficult and oppressive times will make you wise but not rich, and their value lies in their opportunities for discovering the inherent power of faith, self-confidence, hope and neighbourly love once more.

History is filled with examples of nations and countries which started suffering from the undermining effects of too much wealth as they enjoyed increasing levels of prosperity. In the end they went under and disappeared. This makes me think of the story about the two termites. The young one asked the old termite why the termite army didn't simply storm the house where they were living under the foundations. The answer was: "No, we prefer to carry away one grain of sand at a time from every brick, and in the end the house will fall apart by itself."

> Prosperity, success and wealth may easily lead to a dilution of the timeless, positive and beneficial values of life.

A nation or community's building stones consist, as Browning wrote, of the family circle. This truth is a thousand years old. The "grains of sand" keeping them together are the basic values of life: parental and family love, family values, values of faith, and healthy moral principles. In the past these values of life were kept up and reflected in the family by:

- enjoying meals together as a family;
- having family devotions together;
- having family discussions in which the members may differ;

- talking together;
- having family and extended family feasts.

All of these are "grains of sand" which, as Woodridge wrote, form the building blocks of the national house. I wonder, rather sadly, in how many homes these traditions are kept up.

The Christmas season used to be the one great opportunity for families to get together and commemorate the miracle that took place 2000 years ago. Whether this will be so in future depends on how far the termites of prosperity and wealth have succeeded in carrying away the grains of sand from the building blocks of our national house.

I trust that the most important building block, that of family love, will be kept in good repair, in the words of Coleridge, "in times of prosperity, wealth and success as well as in adverse times of trials and tribulations and suppression."

> Blessed is the person who can carry the burden of king and slave equally well and adapt to it, because he will be able to bear suffering and tribulations.
>
> ~ Seneca ~

6

It is better to remember than not to forget

*M*ost authors praise the human memory as a valuable and precious characteristic. Cicero even went as far as to write that man's ability to remember is his greatest treasure and asset. Plutarch stated that the human memory is the most valuable safe-deposit of history as well as of every person's own life history. Ovid also saw the beauty of memory and wrote that it is a most pleasant aspect of the human mind to be able to remember.

Shakespeare joined in the praise of the memory theme, as well as Tupper, Thomas Wilson and others. Alexander Smith and Nietzsche said that without his memory, man would have been closer to the animals. In this they joined in with Cicero's

> That which is bitter to endure, tends to become sweet to remember.

statement that man distinguishes himself from an animal by his ability to reason and remember.

However, Thomas More added, the tragic part was that the older one got, the weaker that faculty became, and the past became equally vague. Ultimately we remember only those events, good or bad, that made an exceptionally strong impression on us or that influenced our lives.

> Man's ability to remember is his greatest treasure and asset.

Some authors have commented on the ironic fact that it is particularly the hardships, sorrow and pain of the past that become some of our best memories. Euripides wrote: "How sweet it is to remember the sorrows and problems of the past!" Authors such as Seneca, Virgil, Fuller, Pollock and Dumas agreed when they wrote that that which was bitter to endure, tended to become sweet to remember. Cowper and Arnold thought back nostalgically in their works about the times when they were so unhappy.

On the other hand, there are authors such as Dante, Robert Blair and Alfred de Musset who contended that past happiness and joy were often painful to recall, especially in difficult times. That is why Shakespeare recommended that, because the needle of memory is so sharp, we should not burden our memory with pain and unpleasantness. Felicia Haman added that to forget is the best ointment for a painful memory, no matter how good the previous times were.

However, Edgar Jones wrote that this is easier said than done, because, whether you have had good or bad experiences, it will take more than all the science in the world to forget them, especially when you want to force yourself to forget.

The statement by Bishop Hugh Latimer that it is better to remember than not to forget, has long interested me, and it has been the subject of heated discussions among acquaintances.

Most of us do not normally see a difference between the two concepts. After all, by remembering, you do not

> Human memory is the most valuable safe-deposit of history.

forget, and, by not forgetting, you remember! Why make such a song and dance about it?

However, in dictionaries the two concepts, "to remember" and "not to forget," are not defined in terms of one another. "Remember" is not defined as "not to forget" and "not to forget" is not defined as "to remember." Furthermore, "to remember" is positive whereas "not to forget" is negative.

In this vein, it has been told that the scientist, Isaac Newton, was very fond of his cat. She always kept him company in his study and whenever she wanted to enter or leave, she would scratch on the door to draw his attention. He regularly had to break his concentration to open the door for her. And then a kitten joined the company and doubled Newton's problem as the mother cat now needed to enter and leave every few minutes, and Newton's work was constantly interrupted. He called in a handyman and directed him to make two holes in the bottom of the door: a large one for the mother cat and a small one for the kitten. "Why?" asked the handyman, "the kitten can just as well use the mother's hole." "True," answered Newton, "but I want the mother to know that I remembered the kitten, as I did the mother, and that I did not forget the kitten." This illustrates the difference between to remember and not to forget.

Another very apt story comes from a European kingdom of hundreds of years ago. The reigning king was getting old and there was no heir to the throne. The royal couple as well as the nation were getting worried about the lack of an heir apparent and a negative atmosphere started growing. And then, at last, it happened! The queen gave birth to their son. The nation was overjoyed. All the citizens took part in the festivities, parties and general merry-making all over the country. Every year afterwards the prince's birthday was celebrated by a week of festivities and it seemed that nothing could suppress the nation's enthusiasm for these events. But slowly the prince himself seemed to lose interest in the goings-on. When his father, the king, one day asked him why he didn't show more interest in the preparations for his own birthday, he answered: "Yes, father, the people show by the festivities that they have not forgotten my birthday, but in the meantime they do not remember me any longer."

Christmas is a delightful time of the year to which everybody looks forward with glad expectations. Preparations for holidays are made, gifts are bought, baking and cooking are done and one can feel the excitement in the air and see the signs of the festive season, because we are celebrating the birthday of the Prince of princes of all times. The atmosphere reminds us not to forget his birthday. Prof. Milan Mahovec of the University of Prague wrote in his book *Jesus for atheists* about the phenomenon that occurred during the 1970s when part of the communist world urgently began searching for and showing interest in the Christ figure, in his ideals and his huge influence in the world over the past two thousand years. Mahovec, an outspoken Marxist, told how he and like-minded persons perceive us as Christians from their perspective; how we by our actions and attitude bring honour to Christ only in words while in our hearts He and his ideals are far away from us; exactly what Jesus said about the Pharisees. Here Mahovec also indicated the shift in emphasis that took place among Christians regarding Christmas. I can imagine Mahovec and his adherents arriving among us at Christmas time and saying: "Enjoy your festivities and parties because you have not forgotten his birthday. But give Him back to us because you don't remember Him any longer. Our festivities will be about Him and not so much about his birthday." That is why Bishop Hugh Latimer wrote the truth: "It is better to remember than not to forget."

Let us remember Him too while we and our loved ones all enjoy a very blessed Christmas. That is my prayer for all of you.

> The human memory is the most valuable safe-deposit of history as well as of every person's own life history.
>
> ~ *Plutarch* ~

7

*P*ositive thinking

*T*his essay considers optimism and positive thinking – related subjects that are talked and written about much these days. We are continually encouraged to be positive and optimistic. This advice is to be welcomed wholeheartedly because a courageous, optimistic and positive approach or attitude in these times is, as Shakespeare so aptly remarked, the most important medicine to carry one through wretchedness and low morale. We cannot enter the new year with pessimism, negativity and discouragement. Too much is at stake: for each of us personally, for our people and for our country. Granted, there certainly are enough problems around us to be uncertain, pessimistic or negative about. However, numerous examples from history confirm that it has always been so, and that even in so-called restful and prosperous times there were people who were pessimistic and discouraged.

The other day I read a paragraph published in the Bloemfontein newspaper, *The friend,* of 5 December 1893: "The exceptionally difficult and demanding times in which we live; our tardy goverment; the weak economy; losses of stock and agricultural products plus the lack of a community feeling among our population are responsible for the ruling discontent and criminal negligence." These are remarks made over a century ago – and they are equally valid today. This is merely yet another substantiation of the biblical statement that there is nothing new under the sun; and that everything that is, has already been. This is also true of our pessimism and negative attitudes. Numerous authors have pointed out that the adverse effects of pessimism and a negative mind are not limited to the afflicted individual, but they spread to his family and other people around him and eventually reach the nation and the country. Chesterton warned that pessimism is like opium: one can get addicted to it. He further stated that it is no medicine, but poison; it is never nourishment for the soul, and is not for people who do things, who build and develop. Christopher added that negativity and pessimism come easily – they arrive automatically – and it takes effort, work and dedication not to succumb. A more modern author, Robert Webster, compared this state of mind with a disease of which the virus spreads easily. That is true: pessimism is catching and it is easy to talk a person into it or to influence him negatively.

It is impossible to quote all the authors who wrote about the characteristics of people with a negative or pessimistic attitude or leaning, but a summary shows that these people usually:

• sit still and do nothing;

- sit and look at others around them;
- feed their own pessimism and negativity by glee-fully pointing out how badly off other people and the country are;
- do nothing but criticise and condemn;
- can see nothing good or beautiful in the people, events, or nature around them;
- are unappreciative about their own good health or prosperity;
- withdraw themselves from the community and their environment and become uninvolved and non-caring;
- are afraid and uncertain and have no self-confidence;
- are faithless and only waiting to die (as Havelock Ellis wrote, "those who insist on lying down be-cause they are paralysed");
- have no perspective and generalise easily, in other words they judge the world situation and that in their country in the light of a single or individual occurrence;
- have no sense of humour.

By contrast, positive thinking and optimism have been praised by most authors from the earliest times, and lauded as a healthy way of life. Optimism, a positive approach and courage indeed become a lifestyle; a way of life that serves as

> Pessimism is not for people who do things, who build and develop.

armour against attacks on body and soul. It has to be learnt by dedication, concentration and hard work, particularly because it is so easy to become pessimistic and negative. We all experience off-days when we do feel a little pessimistic and negative, but that is the time to fight, as Christopher said, the possibility of accepting it as a lifestyle. Baillie stated that courageous people are those who can turn their fears into positive audacity and make challenges of their problems.

> Being positive means to declare under all circumstances that all is well.

An important cornerstone of a positive attitude to life is faith because, as St. Paul wrote, one *must* believe that everything works to the good.

A study of authors' opinions on this matter point to five possible formulae, solutions or recipes to avoid negativity and instead to develop a positive approach and optimism. Once more it is impossible to mention the names of all the authors; I can give only the gist of each argument.

The first solution is to flee or to emigrate to get away from the causes of pessimism or negativity. This solution is criticised by most authors. Ausonius, inter alia, is of the opinion that you only torture yourself by fleeing in order to avoid the problem before you have attempted to confront and overcome it because, according to Thoreau, the final borders of human courage under adverse conditions have rarely been tested. Emerson thought that people fleeing from their problems did so because of fear and ignorance. Most authors agree that one cannot truly get away from one's problems because, as Publilius Syrus stated, at your destination new and possibly greater problems will await you. The devil of negativity will have newer and possibly more poisonous arrows. Fuller added that anybody who did not have a courageous heart, must have fleet feet.

Second is the so-called "balance-sheet" solution in which one is either positive or negative depending on whether positive or negative events dominate the news. Your attitude is constantly yo-yoing up and down along with the news.

Voltaire, Robert Browning, Seneca, Dryden and others agreed, however, that your mind will never be positive as long as it depended on external happenings, because the daily news is saturated with items of death, anguish, violence, conflict, misery and war and they will always be part of daily life. It is wrong, therefore, to be guided only by what is happening in the country. Graham Thomson stated that in spite of everything happening around him, he would still rather live than die, and Longfellow added that one should not fear the world in which one lives because it is an honour to suffer and to be strong and endure.

Third is the so-called "comparative recipe" or solution where you look at your neighbour, and if his situation is as bad or worse, you become more positive. When his situation is better

> Positive thinking is the softest pillow in times of hardship.

than yours, you become negative. Pope and other authors are of the opinion that it is wrong, if not immoral, to found your own positive thinking on the good or bad luck of your neighbour.

In the fourth place one finds the so-called "historical solution" in which positive thinking is built upon the fact that our forebears suffered serious problems but survived in the end. Emerson said that optimism and courage are also to be found in previous suffering that was overcome and survived. That is why the use of history is to give meaning to the present. The authors agree that one can learn positive thinking from

> One should not fear the world in which one lives because it is an honour to suffer and to be strong and endure.

the victories and survivals of the past, and, stated Bierce, "an illustrious past creates the expectation of being positive and optimistic even in a future of problems."

Fifth and certainly the most important solution or recipe to change your attitude to life from negative to positive, is to rely on your own innate power and belief. This is the only solution not dependent on external factors, events or history. Positive thinking is a matter of your own will and cannot depend upon textbooks, symposia and other sources for development – these can only be aids in the process. Voltaire said that being positive means to declare under all circumstances that all is well. Jefferies said that in spite of the frown on his forehead and the wrinkles on his face, he remained an optimist. Robert Browning believed in making the best of the worst. Dryden maintained that courage came from the hearts of people, not from their numbers. Positive thinking and optimism will carry us through anything, believed Sophocles, and Robert Burton wrote that positive thinking was the softest pillow in times of hardship.

Two requirements for positive thinking were identified by the authors. In the first place we must adapt to the circumstances of the day without loss of values, direction and vitality, otherwise, Phaedrus said, you will lose the battle. Virgil said we can and shall win because we must truly believe that we can and shall.

Secondly, according to Emerson, the secret of positive thinking lies in believing in yourself. Positive thinking starts within yourself; and your belief in yourself, said Carlyle, is an acknowledgement of your Creator. Samuel Smiles was of the opinion that optimism is like the sun – as long as we are walking towards the sun, the shadows of negativity and pessimism will fall behind us. Faith in ourselves, according to the unanimous opinion of all the authors, is the only true source of postive thinking. Washington aptly remarked that it is not the size of the *dog* in a fight that makes the difference, it's the size of the *fight!*

When Dorothea Dix was dying of cancer, she said: "Even in my death-bed I can still do something for my fellow man, and that is to be positive and to be an example." One should ask oneself in these times: "What is the alternative for positive thinking and optimism?" It can only be pessimism, negative thoughts and discouragement, along with all the other related attitudes which Antigonus called self-inflicted torture. Fletcher called it an impoverishment of the mind, and Hubbard spoke of a revolting and contagious leprosy. The Bible calls it sinful.

A final thought comes from Everett Hake: "Positive

thinking is not only a mindset but much more. It is a code of conduct; a way of behaviour; and a way to die. It is being human in the fully positive sense of the word; it is always to look up and not down; to look ahead and not back; to look outwards and not inwards and to assist others to do so as well."

I wish you all an absolutely positive year of positive thoughts and optimism – we can if we will.

> Positive thinking is not only a mindset but much more. It is a code of conduct; a way of behaviour; and a way to die. It is being human in the fully positive sense of the word; it is always to look up and not down; to look ahead and not back; to look outwards and not inwards and to assist others to do so as well.
>
> *~ Everett Hake ~*

8

*S*elf-faith and self-confidence

I want to continue the thoughts of the previous essay on positive thinking and optimism, and consider self-confidence and self-faith (created by combinations such as self-control, self-respect, self-complacency and many others). Self-faith is the faith that a person has in himself. Self-faith is an important source of self-confidence. A person with a strong self-faith usually also possesses a strong self-confidence, and according to the author George Herbert the two characteristics in unison form an invincible army in the battle against pessimism and negative thinking.

Some authors draw a comparison with the biblical commandment that measures your love for your neighbour according to your love for yourself. In the same way, they aver, will the strength of your self-faith determine the strength of your self-confidence.

Ovid stated that nothing can stand in your way if you really believe in yourself. Higgins agreed and added that self-faith should be pure and strong, like true love, and if it is not so – should you not truly believe in yourself – nothing you attempt will be successful. Thomas Fuller asked: "How can a half-hearted and superficial self-faith ever ensure success and victory?" Likewise, Bernard Shaw asked: "How on earth can you expect anyone to believe in you if you do not believe in yourself?" Seneca wrote that what you think of yourself is usually more important than what others think of you. Martin agreed, using the following words: "When you really believe in yourself, you find that it becomes all the more difficult to doubt yourself." Lamartine added that self-faith and self-confidence grow and become stronger, and Tertullian said that anything that may seem impossible to the ordinary person becomes possible to you. Nobody can make you believe in yourself – self-faith is a personal matter – only you, and you alone, can make it happen, warned Daniel Webster.

> Self-faith and self-confidence form an invincible army in the battle against pessimism.

Strong self-faith gives birth to self-confidence and feeds it. Self-confidence is the foundation of success and fulfilment. That is why a lack of self-confidence is more often than not the reason for many of our problems.

Many authors accentuate the importance of self-confidence in our relationships, in our behaviour, in our daily actions. Samuel Johnson was convinced that self-confidence is the prerequisite for any great deed or enterprise that you wish to attempt. Cicero said that, provided your self-confidence is strong enough, you are

bound to be successful. Samuel Johnson further believed that your remuneration
would be equal to the confidence that you showed in
yourself. Samuel Cole em-
phasised the point that you

> Nothing can stand in your way if you really believe in yourself.

are in charge of your own fate, saying that "not fate,
not luck, nor the stars, but solely your own self-confidence will determine your success." Cicero wrote that
he who depends on himself, is lucky, and Montaigne
wrote that he learned that all his hope in everything
that he attempted, was to be found in his self-faith and
self-confidence.

Emerson, along with other authors, saw self-confidence as an essentially human characteristic when he
wrote that self-confidence was the essence of bravery.
Livy wrote that the stronger your confidence in yourself is, the more you will stimulate self-confidence in
others.

People with self-confi-
dence think *big,* or more glo-
bally. Chamberlain's advice
was to think and believe
universally (or imperially)
and Grenville Kleiser said
that how we think and be-
lieve, determines the greatness or limitations of our
world.

> You may lose anything in life except your self-faith and your self-con-fidence because, should you lose those, your self-respect and your pride in yourself will be gone as well, and then you will think nothing of yourself.

People with a strong self-
faith and self-confidence usually also have high ideals.

Haydon stated that it *must* be so, because any person who does not want to do better than only good enough, will cause his self-faith and self-confidence to rust and deteriorate. Sir Henry Taylor averred that nothing will compel a person to action if he does not couple his self-confidence with ideals.

> Nothing will compel a person to action if he does not couple his self-confidence with ideals.

Young added that he who builds under the stars, builds too low. Lucan believed that by thinking great, fear will be conquered.

Think tall is a poem by James Beaumont that I like to read. It basically says that if you *think* you will lose, you have *already* lost, and if you *think* you will fail, you have *already* failed. Victory and success are matters of thought and faith. Self-confidence, and not luck determine our success. Victory and success are not always for the strong and great, but for every person who thinks and believes that he can.

Errors in our lives become one of the strongest reasons for a lack of self-confidence, because self-faith and self-confidence are such important building blocks in determining success and triumph. Bernard Shaw said that nothing is as simple as breaking down another's self-confidence. Franklin agreed, saying that nothing is as deadly as undermining another person's self-confidence. Errors are unavoidable but still necessary as part of life. They make you stumble and sometimes even fall and every time your self-confidence is bashed. However, Mary Pickford wrote that the problem was perhaps not the fall, but staying down! By getting up, your self-confidence ought to be boosted so that it would be better than before the fall. One should get up and not allow your self-confidence to evaporate in the end because, according to Robert Browning, the systematic destruction of your self-confidence can cause it never to be healed again.

What I have said about self-confidence and self-faith for the individual is equally applicable to a group or a nation. A nation that has no faith in itself and no self-confidence, or that allows them to be systematically and continuously destroyed, is on the way to total destruction. No group or nation can therefore afford to allow continuous reproaches and blame to be flung at its head for mistakes or errors committed in the past. Washington wrote, "You may lose anything in life except your self-faith and your self-confidence because, should you lose those, your self-respect and your pride in yourself will be gone as well, and then you will think nothing of yourself." Dryden wrote that a guilty conscience is poisonous and it makes a coward of a person. Seneca said that the lack of faith and self-confidence is not the result of problems, but much rather it is the other way round: the problems follow on a lack of self-faith and self-confidence.

> Nobody can make you believe in yourself – self-faith is a personal matter – only you, and you alone, can make it happen.
>
> *~ Daniel Webster ~*

9

The human tongue

Over thousands of years many sayings have developed and originated around the human tongue – an organ that to this day captivates the attention of medical science with its mobility, agility and other unique abilities and characteristics.

The human tongue plays a key role in most spheres of the community: trade, politics, amusement, law, and religion, to name but a few. And naturally, the ability to taste lies at the foundation of the catering business worldwide. Without his tongue man would not have been nearly what he is now, and nor would the world. That is one reason why the most gruesome of attacks on a human is the removal of his tongue. Emerson maintained that his tongue was what differentiated man from an animal.

The tongue's ability to speak, and the results thereof form the central theme of many poems. The human tongue is praised,

> It is a musical instrument without strings that makes music more beautiful than birdsong.

lauded and celebrated as the organ wihout which mankind could never have developed as far as it did. Numerous pleasures, joys and happy experiences would have had to have been gone without. Hesiod wrote that it is the most important asset of the human being without which none of the praise songs in the Psalms

> Without his tongue man would not have been nearly what he is now, and nor would the world.

would ever have been sung, and, said Cowper, nor would the gospels have been written or told.

The authors Thomas Fuller, John Davies, Cicero, Seneca and others each in his own way bring praise to the human tongue and the positive role that it played in history. Davies summarised their consensus that the tongue has accomplished much more than the strongest hand. Wordsworth said that the human tongue could touch and stir the deeps of man; Johnson spoke about the most tender love that can be transmitted from person to person; and Woodrow Wilson stated that it could create the most perfect harmony.

Proverbs 15:4 says, "The tongue that brings healing is a tree of life," and Shakespeare spoke about its unknown, breathtaking magic and its gift of making crying people laugh and the sad ones glad; it is a musical instrument without strings that makes music more beautiful than bird-song. Shakespeare would that his tongue had the strength of lightning, so that he could enchant the whole earth with passion. Fuller described the tongue as both the sails and the helm of the human ship of life.

These are but a few of the songs of praise to the

human tongue and its achievements to be found in poetry and other manuscripts.

However, there is another side as well; in the words of Laertes, there is just as much bad as good in the tongue. Plautus referred to the tongue as the fool's

> Do not allow your tongue to anticipate your brain.

greatest asset. Bulwer-Lytton warned that it is in the magic of the split tongue that the greatest danger lurks. Job 20:12 warns: "Evil is sweet in his mouth and he hides it under his tongue." Therefore, be warned, it is an organ that can change without pause from situation to situation. Claudius wrote about the pure white angel-robe that is discarded in a second to bring forth a fiery satan sowing sorrow, pain, destruction and even death from the darkest depths of hate and venom.

This unpredictable and huge potential for uncontrollability in the daily life fills authors with both admiration and real fear. That is where all the comparisons to dangerous, deceptive and destructive characteristics and behaviour come from.

In James 3 the tongue is described as an unruly evil; Psalm 52 mentions a deceitful tongue. Shakespeare compared a flattering but deceitful tongue with the wagging tail of a treacherous dog. Several authors agreed that, although the tongue does not have a

> The first part of the human body to be controlled, is the tongue.

sharp edge, it can cut to the deeps: it is a weapon sharper than the sword. John Wycliffe quoted from the apocryphical books a saying that where a whip leaves marks only on the body, the tongue will break hearts and bones.

Quarles remarked that an unwise word from you was the same as giving your sword to your enemy. The irony is that the tongue, which causes the most grief, does not get tired and remains unhurt itself. It does not tire easily and does not get worn out, but, said Irving, it gets sharper as times passes!

Tarton and Hawkes noted that the tongue has a remarkable capacity to turn a secret into news – the moment that a secret lands on the tip of the tongue it becomes common property. The tongue must be kept away from a secret or the secret will lose its character. And therefore, wrote Logan, a quiet tongue is the characteristic of a wise person on whom you can depend.

> A flattering but deceitful tongue is like the wagging tail of a treacherous dog.

It is due to this split nature of the tongue that there are so many warnings about the human tongue. Psalm 34:13 warns you to keep your tongue from evil, and authors such as Chilon, Fuller, Franklin, Emerson and others warn you to think before you talk. Herbert stated succinctly: "Do not allow your tongue to anticipate your brain." Fuller added that a mistake made by hands and feet can usually be rectified, but the results of a slip of the tongue are irrevocable.

Against this background Chaucer and Hoskins recommended that the first part of the human body to be controlled, is the tongue – even before a child learns to talk, if possible.

Silence is golden and that is why, said Cicero, a knowledgeable but quiet tongue is to be preferred to a talking tongue that may merely reveal ignorance. Dionysius Cato even said that he who knew how to control his tongue is at that moment nearest to God.

Colton wrote in *Lacon:* when a person is talking in a reasonable fashion, his tongue is working in harmony with his brain, eyes, ears and heart. Then all the parts of the body will act in synergy, and the tongue will be controlled and in symphony with the rest.

However, Cowper wrote that this nimble and mobile organ often acted like a poisonous viper spewing forth its poison of deceit and evil into the world. Gracián said: "That is the moment when the tongue becomes an untamed animal bursting through the bars of civilised control to sow discord and trouble." Shakespeare and Voltaire agreed that we all know that what we are about to say may be wrong or false, but we allow the tongue to carry on with the process of hurting and humiliating.

This is where the old value of life is proved: where self-control ends, self-humiliation begins.

> When a person is talking in a reasonable fashion, his tongue is working in harmony with his brain, eyes, ears and heart. Then all the parts of the body will act in synergy, and the tongue will be controlled and in symphony with the rest.
>
> ~ *Charles Caleb Colton* ~

10

*R*emorse,
self-reproach
and self-crucifixion

he values of life around the concepts remorse, self-reproach and self-crucifixion are usually confused and used as synonyms, but in reality they are essentially different. We often hear the words "if only I had said this or that," or, "if we could only turn back the clock, matters would have been so different and mistakes could have been avoided." The list of regrets

> Self-reproach inexorably leads to self-crucifixion.

about things past is endless. We all have them and we would all love to have them erased so that they cease to exist. We also have the very best intentions of never, but never, doing those things again.

Let us look at the three different concepts. The first is regret: to be sorry about making the wrong decision, or about something we said or did that we should have avoided. George Eliot wrote: "It is human to err and have proper remorse over it; that remorse will be as a resurrection after a death – the beginning of a new life." Franklin Adams thought that the words, "I am sorry, I regret what I have done," are the most beautiful words you can say to yourself; they cleanse your spirit. The modern German author Klaus Benge compared remorse with a hot bath: the deeper the remorse, the warmer the water and the cleaner or more pure your spirit. Homer and Cowper wrote that remorse was essential because it was like the death of an old body and the beginning of a new life. It is self-reformation. However, some warnings should be heeded: do not go further than regretting your wrong deeds and asking forgiveness after feeling true remorse. It is wrong to carry this to the second phase,

> Remorse, self-reproach and self-crucifixion are essentially different.

which is to keep on reproaching yourself endlessly. Self-reproach becomes a negative burden if you keep on carrying it when you should have left it behind you. Addison wrote: "Self-reproach is one of the worst burdens that you can lay on your heart," and Thomas Gray said: "Self-reproach means looking back too long, so that you do not look ahead, and then you run the risk of making the same mistake or a worse error." To err is like falling, and to reproach yourself for too long is to keep lying in the dust.

Whittier, Thoreau and others argued that the most destructive and repetitive words you can direct at yourself are: "It could have been so different." Longfellow grieved about the joyful days and hours that we waste in self-reproach while life runs past us, and Byron and Robinson wrote about the ever-burning and all-consuming fire of self-reproach in the heart, which, according to Congreve, eats away at the depths of the heart.

> Life and the future are too precious to spoil with self-reproach.

Many authors warn that the self-reproach that you are carrying and pampering inexorably leads to the third phase, that of self-crucifixion. This happens when you keep on reproaching yourself long enough to destroy your mind and ultimately your body. Shakespeare compared self-reproach with the poison of a scorpion: it burns and hurts and whenever it is awakened by remembering, it will start hurting again just as poignantly. In the end it destroys, until you wish that you were never born.

Kierkegaard's opinion is that we know and understand the past because it is done with: it is now part of our experience and knowledge to use; we have lived through it. But the future lies ahead: it must still be lived and there is no room for morbid souls carrying self-inflicted judgments over mistakes committed in the past. Samuel Johnson wrote: "Life demands from us to go into the future without the unnecessary baggage of self-reproach." "For the happy, cheerful and committed person life is always

> To err is like falling, and to reproach yourself for too long is to keep lying in the dust.

too short, but for those who prefer to drag their burden of self-reproach along, life is exhausting and seems eternal," said Lucian.

Rossetti put it very well: "To err is human and to regret it and have remorse over it is imperative for the cleansing of the soul." Then you must close it like a book and put it away in the library of your experiences and memories where you may want to look it up sometimes to refresh your mind with the lessons to be learnt therein. "However, to walk about with self-reproach and overlong regrets in your heart, is the way of a coward," said Alan Defoe.

Life and the future are gifts of God, too precious to spoil with self-reproach about the past.

William Darling wrote: "Regretting and feeling remorse about past mistakes is like an offering at life's altar: your heart is infused with peace and you can start from the beginning." But the person who crucifies himself at the altar of life will not only be consumed in the altar fire, but he also does not understand the message of love and hope of a crucifixion almost 2000 years ago. The ultimate price has been paid there already.

> The words, "I am sorry, I regret what I have done," are the most beautiful words you can say to yourself; they cleanse your spirit.
>
> ~ Franklin Adams ~

11

*F*ear and anguish

*F*ear is a human and mostly negative emotion experienced in times of stress, threat or danger. Numerous values of life about fear are to be found in the manuscripts of modern as well as antique authors. Cowper wrote that all of us experience fear and anguish. Yes, agreed Tacitus, even the bravest and most courageous know fear.

Many authors pointed out the difference between positive (good) and negative (bad) fear. However, most of them agreed that there is more danger than good in any form of fear. Fear is mostly detrimental to anyone. Froude said that fear is usually the father of cruelty and Emerson wrote that it is usually the child of ignorance. Syrus stated that fear always stands in the way of all virtues, and Statius wrote that idolatry was historically born of fear, and that fear was the worst prophet of the future. Voltaire main-

> Fear can be conquered.

tained that fear was the worst punishment for crime and sin. Shakespeare thought that treason often has its origin in fear – it makes traitors of us. He added that to fear, is to fall and lose. Lord Chesterfield believed that fear was an invitation to danger.

A few authors painted an even worse picture of fear. Cicero wrote that ultimately no human power could stand fast against the weight of fear, and Fuller

> Fear must lead to the good.

said that fear was much stronger than love. Fear is incurable because no medicine, herbs or spices can cure it, and Nichols described fear as the highest fence of our mind. Bernard Shaw believed that fear will drive one to the utmost, and Coelius Rufus said that it made one believe the worst.

However, other authors believed that the importance of fear is exaggerated and that it can be conquered. Defoe stated that the fear is often worse than the thing that is feared and Stevenson suggested that one should keep one's fear to oneself and share one's courage. The authors Livy and Hubbard stated that what we fear, may easily happen to us, which is why we can reduce the danger by reducing the fear. Alexander wrote that self-confidence and faith will dispel fear. Syrus said: "If you know how to control your fear, you will also know how to go through life."

A number of authors stressed the relationship

> Fear is human.

between fear, hope and hate. Quintius Ennius said that one fears those that one hates. Ovid said that this is why one would like to see those that one hates, destroyed. Robert Browning wrote that the recognition of fear comes from hope, and La Roché said that fear and hope are irrevocably joined – no fear without hope and no hope without fear. Seneca wrote that it must be terrible to fear without hope, and Scott thought that hope shines brightest when it comes out from behind a cloud of fear.

The Bible refers to instances of both bad and good fear. Numerous verses admonish us not to fear, but to go forth in the fear of the Lord. The author of Proverbs stated: "Happy is the man who fears." An anonymous author agreed: "Fear is the foundation of obedience to Him and as such of a holy and pure life on earth." However, the Bible also teaches us not to fear negatively, as in the clear directive in Proverbs: "Do not fear – not the water of a raging river nor the devouring flame of the fire."

> Fear and hope are irrevocably joined – no fear without hope and no hope without fear.

Numerous authors, inter alia Unamuno, focused on the positive side of fear: "Wisdom is often born of fear." Cowper said, "He who has never feared, cannot know hope." Herbert wrote: "Fear is often the origin of hope." As long as we believe in our project with a good measure of fear, we will never lack for courage.

Lanz argued that the question is: "To fear or not to fear." Tertius's response was, "No, that is not the question, because to fear is human, essential and inevitable." Fear must lead to the good; it must be positive, giving rise to prayer, devotion, respect, discipline and neighbourly love. Orderly living in a community is also based on healthy fear. Here we once more find the bond between fear and hope, because fear for authority gives us hope for an orderly community. Remove the positive fear, and the hope for law and order in the community will disappear, which will heighten the hate. When negative fear takes over it leads to a hopeless situation in which the bush law of tooth and claw conquers. Anacharsis wrote: "It is pure anguish to fear something against which the citizen stands helpless."

It is absurd, wrote Publilius Syrus, to fear something that is inevitable, natural and human. Our enemies are not hardships, age, change in our country and our lives, or even death: these are inevitable, natural and human. Our enemy is much rather our fear – our anguish – about these inevitable events in our lives. Thoreau put it so well: "One should fear fear: one must be afraid of being afraid and have anguish for anguish." That is the way to triumph over negative fears.

> Hope shines brightest when it comes out from behind a cloud of fear.
>
> ~ *Scott* ~

12

$\mathcal{F}$rom retaliation to reconciliation

$\mathcal{V}$alues about retaliation (revenge or punishment), making excuses (apologising), forgiveness and reconciliation show an interesting line of development from antique times to the year 2000. The development shows that in antique times a crime against the state, the government, community or an individual was without exception punished in a suitable way. However, in modern times the accent has shifted, and Bentham even wrote that in contemporary society it is almost regarded as an evil to punish the guilty.

William Gaynor's opinion is likewise that the world does not gain by punishment and that the constable's baton improves nothing.

The so-called *talio* principle – an eye for an eye and a tooth for a tooth, as stated in the Bible – used to prevail. Authors such as Ovid, Seneca and Phaedrus wrote that the criminal was to be punished with death or banishment from the community, the loss of a limb or another punishment befitting the crime. The retaliation was hard and cruel. The accent was on the criminal, his deed and his punishment: you reaped what you sowed. There was very little if any room for excuses or apologies. As far as is known, the retaliatory system was applied in the antique civilisations' legal systems and communities. As far back as 2100 BC the laws of Hammurabi, section 196, stipulated as follows: "An eye for an eye." Tibullus said that by this retaliatory principle misdeeds were punished, order was maintained, peace was kept and communities developed.

> The cycle from retaliation to reconciliation is completed.

In certain countries this principle still prevails, and a criminal must feel the punishment for his wrongdoing on his body: a thief's hand is cut off, for example. And, in those countries, there is almost no theft.

Wilandt was of the opinion that retaliation as compensator and educator was possibly exaggerated in antique times, but it is true that up to the beginning of the 20th century it did ensure stability in the most primitive communities.

Alfieri's opinion is that criminals must be punished irrespective of the person, because law-abiding and innocent citizens must at all times be protected and feel safe, whereas the guilty must be exposed and punished. Tacitus said: "In this respect the nature of man and an animal is the same: a

> In contemporary society it is almost regarded as an evil to punish the guilty.

mistake in the animal world leads to the death of the transgressor." In antique times the government, community and individual were so strongly focused on retaliation that even an insult could lead to the death of the perpetrator, and many a person who possibly had a very good reason for his behaviour, lost a limb or was banned.

Nobody is quite sure of when exactly the apologetic or reconciliatory phase started. The new approach was: give the accused a chance to state his case and why he should not receive the fitting punishment. This approach is still in use in the law systems of all civilised countries and is called the *audi alteram partem* rule. This principle softened the hearts of governments and citizens alike and Plautus

> Phase 1: Offenders reaped what they sowed.

mentioned that the eye for an eye and tooth for a tooth principle was watered down. Slowly but surely the apologetic and reconciliatory principle took over with an altogether more humane way of punishment. The crime remained a fact, but the retaliation principle was being replaced by the reconciliation principle. However, Seneca and Alfieri wrote that it was still necessary to punish the criminal. In certain circumstances the punishment was diminished. The accent was still on punishment, but with possible mitigation.

The third phase started with the coming of Christ and the Christian religion at the beginning of our era. Forgiveness was introduced. The authors Meredith, Hubbard and Cohen refer to it as the "turn-your-cheek" approach of which we read in the Bible. During this transitional time forgiveness started taking over from revenge. Bohn and Ray said that forgiveness became the most noble form of revenge, and Palmer said if one added a smile it made the revenge even better!

The shift in emphasis from retaliation (or revenge) to conciliation (or apology) and from there to forgiveness is reflected in the statements of many authors. Bailey wrote that the more you forgave, the more would be forgiven you, and

> Phase 2: Give the accused a chance to state his case.

an anonymous author wrote that the person who could not forgive, would die unforgiven. William Smith, Herbert and others quote certain classical authors to support the viewpoint that retaliation or revenge are characteristic of barbarism and that forgiveness is better than punishment. Smith said that forgiveness is heavenly. Bentham and William Gaynor agreed that punishment was evil and that retaliation or punishment for a crime did not make the world a better place. It is human to err and heavenly to forgive and therefore forgiveness is better than punishment. Forgiveness for transgressions and crimes became the norm: the perpetrator only had to say he was sorry. However, Oliver Wendell Holmes said it was all very well that apology became fashionable, but it restored nothing.

In the meantime, though, nothing stood still, as usual. The impact of the Second World War and developments afterwards brought about the equalising phase between criminal and proper deeds, right and wrong, guilt and innocence, and retaliation and conciliation. We must reconcile ourselves with the phenomenon of crime, is the approach of the time in which we now live. The guilt for a misdeed is no longer seen to belong to the perpetrator, but lies in the factors surrounding him: his circumstances, background, drunkenness, uncontrollable temper, aggression, loneliness, natural impulses and many other, according to Asquith, beautiful arguments for very serious misdeeds and very gruesome acts.

The author Mencken believes that forgiveness is no longer necessary: it has now become acceptance or "living with it" because good and bad, right and wrong are all the same. Time makes all things equal.

Cohen and Hagan wrote (with reference to Juvenal and Seneca): "The day will come that if you want to be someone important, you will have to commit a crime that justifies banning or a gaol sentence, or a crime that is profitable or popular. It becomes a virtue; apologies, excuses and even forgiveness no longer play a role." Milton said they had become cheap and irrelevant commodities. Meredith said that, should you ask for forgiveness, you would be regarded as maladjusted and be insulted. Shakespeare said that the danger was that we so easily asked for forgiveness and were pardoned with such facility that there ceased to be any meaning in the acts; we have been reconciled to crime and have forsaken retaliation.

Phase 3: Forgiveness; turn the other cheek.

The cycle from retaliation to reconciliation is completed. Where it will end, only the future will show.

Authors such as Inglesworth, Cohen and Rembert pointed to the dangers of a government that is so reconciled to crime that it abdicates its responsibilities or neglects to protect its citizens, maintain order and keep the peace. In such a society:

- the community has accepted crime to such a degree that it experiences it passively and as a normal phenomenon;
- murder has become merely a deed of elimination;
- theft, corruption and dishonesty have become achievements;
- the rape of women and child-battering have merely become expressions of natural impulses;
- crime is seen as creating jobs for criminals and therefore is regarded as to the advantage of the country.

Then there is a movement to a new "democracy"; a democracy in which:

- crime is the norm and the culture;
- the minority, the law-abiding citizens, are subject to the dictators of crime;
- the individual is forced to take the law into his own hands;
- anarchy rules.

This may very well be the prelude to strong retaliation in a new dispensation.

It is human to err and heavenly to forgive and therefore forgiveness is better than punishment.

~ Jeremy Bentham and William Gaynor ~

13

*C*hange

*T*hese days we often say that the changes in the world and especially in South Africa take place too rapidly, they are too comprehensive and too unfriendly. Many people do not like these changes and see them as detrimental, if not downright dangerous, and unholy. The changes are far beyond the framework of what they had expected in the new South Africa, and therefore many believe that, as it says in Job, the earth has been delivered to the power of evil and everything that is bad, and before our eyes a shadow of death is coming.

Since 1994 South Africa has increasingly been set free from its previous isolation, and as a consequence our country has also been increasingly exposed to the fast and naturally huge scope of changes in the in-

> This kind of withdrawal is an escape from tension and stress.

ternational world. In the past those changes had reached us fairly slowly and usually quite some time after they started elsewhere. The fast pace of the present changes makes many people feel uncertain and even afraid. Because of this confusion people tend to stick their heads in the sand; to escape into isolation, segregation and withdrawal from everything around them. They:

- no longer read the papers because they contain only bad news;
- no longer watch TV;
- do not listen to the radio because the language and music on it are strange;
- do not read this or that magazine because it only contains sensationalist and unpleasant articles;
- do not care a hoot what happens to the country or their fellow man; it is now each for himself and the devil takes the hindmost.

> For survival we have to be involved with everything around us.

Lots of people don't like what is happening around them. That is why they withdraw from the community and their fellow man. Byron said that this kind of withdrawal is an escape from tension and stress. Job 29 describes it as a longing for times past, when life seemed stable and comforting. This escape to isolation, or withdrawal into oneself, is dangerous, said Byron. You do not need to withdraw yourself from the events of daily life to guard your values, faith, identity, honour and pride. Indeed, said Lord Denning, by isolating yourself you run the risk of losing those valuables.

> Since 1994, our country has also been increasingly exposed to the fast and naturally huge scope of changes in the international world.

It is all about interest and involvement in daily events

and changes in life and in the world, in your community and in your fellow man and his experiences. Many authors agree that withdrawal is highly undesirable and that it leads to isolation and misery.

> Experience the worse parts of life along with the better.

Shakespeare wrote that lack of interest in the community and your fellow man made life pointless, and Revelation 3 speaks about being lukewarm; neither cold nor hot. Menander and Hazlitt said that if you are not interested in other people and your surroundings, you will gradually stop being interested in yourself as well. Laertes believed that for survival we have to be involved with everything around us. Epictetus said that to truly come to know yourself, you have to use your community as a mirror to see yourself, and that can be done only by full participation.

> You do not need to withdraw yourself from the events of daily life.

Murder, theft, corruption, dishonesty, bribery, transgression of moral norms and other misdemeanors and trespasses have always been part of the community. Manuscripts by numerous authors tell about the terrible things that happened in their communities.

One may want to protest and claim that today's events are worse than ever. Pickworth wrote that most of our opinions are based on perceptions; therefore everything is relative. The Bible says several times that everything that has been, will be again, and what happened, will happen again. There is absolutely nothing new under the sun. Indeed, Juvenal wrote 2000 years ago that if you wanted to be in fashion at that time, you only had to commit a crime that would lead to banishment or a gaol sentence. Seneca, another Latin author, also stated that a crime (in his time) that would draw sympathy could be made a virtue by public opinion and turn the criminal into a hero.

It is usually not the crime that determines the range of the punishment and censure, but rather who committed it.

We must not isolate ourselves from world events or events in our own country, or our fellow humans' experiences. It is necessary to read your newspaper regularly, to watch TV, listen to the radio and hear about the misery and anguish of others so that we may share in their joy as well.

Partaking in societies, community activities and other forms of organisational life keeps you posted as to the activities in your neighbourhood and contributes to your continued development. It offers that golden opportunity to give a helping hand to a needy person. That is reason enough to experience the worse parts of life along with the better. And we must not, like Job, yearn for the good times of the past so that the future leaves us behind in the process. It is no good trying to fill the future with the good of the past.

St. Paul and authors such as Radcliffe and Hancke agreed: for our own sake and for what we are, and for our country's sake and what we believe, and for the sake of our fellow humans, we must be interested and take part in the daily events around us and in the outside world. If we do not do so, we will neglect our duty to Him who 2000 years ago gave us this assignment: "You must share in this world if you want to change it."

> To truly come to know yourself, you have to use your community as a mirror to see yourself, and this can be done only by full participation.
>
> ~ Epictetus ~

14

*L*oneliness and isolation

riedland's statement in his book *The denial of insignificance* that there is a difference between isolation and loneliness fascinated my imagination to such an extent that I went to a lot of trouble to find books on this issue.

There is a general perception that many single persons and senior citizens are isolated and therefore lonely and that they become more so as time passes. Most dictionaries describe loneliness and isolation as synonyms and do not recognise a difference.

> The "only" will always be in the lonely heart.

To me it was an exceptionally interesting piece of research that produced a variety of viewpoints. Most authors differentiate between loneliness, a man-made segregation on the one hand, and solitariness, aloneness or being "set apart" on the other. The latter is a unique situation that indicates the origin, the source or eternity; thus a divine or superhuman situation. In that sense it is impossible for a human being to be truly alone because, as Thomas Browne wrote, "God alone is 'unique', the source and beginning," and John Erskine wrote, "it all started with that being 'alone'." Man can only be lonely, said Joseph Cooke, and in that situation there is always one with him, the One that is the "only" one, that is God, according to Joseph Roux. He wrote that the "only"

> Loneliness is a source of joy, triumph, comfort, understanding and sympathy.

will always be in the lonely heart. Andrew Marvell wrote that the Creator was and is unique and always alone. Then He made man who was also alone until He said in Genesis 2:18 that it is not good for the only man to be alone; He would make a helpmeet for him. Eve was also alone until the snake beguiled her. Marvell's opinion is that man was solitary from that moment. Chaucer and Hoccleve believed that loneliness overcame humans from that time and that is why, as is written in Ecclesiastes 4:10, man needs someone to pick him up when he falls.

Loneliness has, for some authors, a negative and depressing meaning. George Meredith described loneliness as the source of suspicion and distrust, and Seneca wrote that loneliness encouraged temptation and beguilement, because, when Eve was alone, the devil beguiled her and, to get rid of her loneliness, she in her turn beguiled Adam. Milton was more moderate when

> Loneliness promotes clarity of mind.

he said that the lonely person usually did not know what joy was and was unable to share it. Samuel Johnson's judgment was sharper when he stated that the lonely person could quite possibly be insane.

Other authors – fortunately most of those whose works I read – are much more positive about loneliness. It is true that a human being is a social animal; he likes mixing with other people and looks for company, but there are times when he appreciates a little privacy, or to be alone. Hamerton's opinion is that man's fear of loneliness is unfounded. Emerson wrote that loneliness is essential for a person, because poverty and isolation are two of the best teachers of true life values. The more profound the loneliness, the sharper the human spirit's development will be. Joseph Roux believes loneliness promotes clarity of mind. Hawthorne also believed in the cleansing power set free by loneliness: the lonely spirit will become inviolate and

> Those who are alone communicate with angels.

unprofaned. Therefore you should often isolate yourself in order to look into your heart and mind, suggested George Herbert. It is wonderful to be alone; away from the masses' noise and rush; away to the silence of isolation; only yourself with loneliness as your spirit's best friend. Goldsmith, Harris and Charles Cotton agreed that there was nothing better. In that isolation you still have the very best company: your own. Loneliness is the caretaker of enthusiasm which in its turn is the father of genius, wrote Disraeli. Wordsworth and Sterne agreed that much wisdom is born in isolation. Henrik Ibsen stated that the most resourceful and influential people are mostly lonely. They usually avoid crowds and although they may often be among people, they never become part of the crowds. Epicurus wrote that these leaders often seek out loneliness. Alice Meynell maintained that, although there can never be loneliness in solitariness (divinity), there is always to be found solitariness (a unique quality, divine inspiration) in loneliness. Sir Philip Sidney and Fletcher wrote that those who are alone or isolated with pure thoughts, communicate with angels on a celestial level because in your isolation your Creator will communicate with you. Stuart Black agreed. Do not think that by locking your door, darkening your room and feeling that you are alone, you are alone with yourself, because you are not: He who is truly alone, is with you, always with you, wrote Epictetus. Landor called loneliness God's consulting room.

Loneliness, isolation and to be totally alone sometimes is a source of many positive, advantageous and essential things; a source of powerful inner strength. Francis Bacon called it a source of joy, triumph, comfort, understanding and sympathy. Rainer wrote that loneliness or isolation is probably the only way to exercise introspection: to take an honest look at yourself and conduct a quiet, frank and sincere discussion with yourself. And you will never be alone in that conversation because of Him who is ever alone, the only One who is the One with you in your loneliness. He will listen to your sorrow but also share in your joy; He will advise you and lead you on the way ahead and keep you safe through the crowds. In the Bible you will find numerous examples of this kind of conversation held in isolation. You can look them up for yourself.

To be always lonely is not good for a human being, because everybody needs his fellow man, but periodic isolation is essential. It is:

- therapy for the spirit;
- a visit to the compass room of the life-book to determine your direction;
- the mountain peak to find your view and perspective;
- the short private stroll through the garden of life for a quiet moment and meditation.

Many authors agree on these points. Loneliness is for the mind what fasting is for the body.

> Therefore you should often isolate yourself in order to look into your heart and mind.
>
> ~ George Herbert ~

* Mwari haanyadzisi nokuti anotaura chokwadi.
* What the Lord says he'll do, he'll do.
* When he says fear not I am with you he means he's with you
# When he says ask and you will receive he means he will give you.
# When he says he will come again, he means he is coming again.
* Ishe haanyepi anotaura idi